KOS TRAVEL GUIDE 2024

Explore the Rich Culture and Beauty of Kos

GW00469719

MONA MURRY

TABLE OF CONTENT

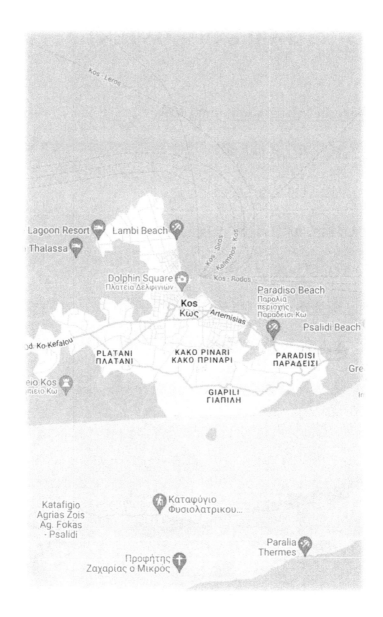

4

INTRODUCTION

Welcome to the enchanting island of Kos, where ancient history blends with olive orchards' soothing flutter and the Aegean Sea's turquoise embrace. In "KOS TRAVEL GUIDE 2024," we encourage you to go on an extraordinary adventure that takes you beyond the pages of a guidebook and immerses you in Kos' soul-stirring magnificence.

Unveiling the essence of Kos

Kos, located in the Dodecanese archipelago, is more than simply an island; it's a living canvas filled with the brushstrokes of mythology, culture, and natural beauty. As you read through the pages of this book, prepare to learn the mysteries of Kos, as each chapter invites you to discover a new aspect of this Aegean treasure.

Why Kos? A glimpse inside your island adventure.

Ancient Echoes: Walk in the footsteps of Hippocrates, the founder of medicine, as you discover the ancient Asklepion and hear the sounds of a bygone period that resound across the island's historical landmarks.

Sandy Serenity: Give in to the appeal of immaculate beaches that extend like ribbons down the coastline, tempting you to bask in the Greek sun, participate in water activities, and relax to the peaceful symphony of lapping waves.

Cultural Mosaic: Immerse yourself in Kos' vivid tapestry of culture, which combines Byzantine, Ottoman, and Venetian influences to create a mosaic of traditions, gastronomic pleasures, and friendly hospitality.

Natural beauty: Travel through landscapes embellished with verdant valleys, craggy mountains, and lush plains, with each turn revealing the island's natural beauty and biodiversity.

Contemporary amenities, Timeless Charm: Discover the ideal balance of contemporary amenities and timeless charm as you tour busy marketplaces, quaint towns, and sophisticated resorts that cater to every traveler's needs.

What to Expect in "KOS TRAVEL GUIDE 2024"

Comprehensive insights: Explore the heart of Kos with in-depth insights into its history, culture, and prominent attractions, ensuring that you not only visit but also thoroughly understand the island.

Practical Travel Recommendations: Use practical transit, lodging, and local customs recommendations to make your trip to Kos more enjoyable.

Designed Itineraries: Whether you're a history buff, a beach lover, or a foodie, find designed itineraries that cater to your interests, assuring a unique vacation.

Hidden jewels: Discover hidden jewels and off-the-beaten-path treasures that add authenticity to your Kos experience, offering moments of discovery away from the crowd.

Your Passport to Unforgettable Moments

As you turn the pages of "KOS TRAVEL GUIDE 2024," imagine yourself meandering amid ancient agora ruins, experiencing the aromas of local food, and losing sight of time on sun-kissed beaches. This book is about more than simply locations; it's about creating memories that will make you fall in love with Kos, one experience at a time.

Embark on Your Kos Odyssey Today!

This guide is more than just a book; it's a companion, a storyteller, and a doorway into the heart of Kos. Don't only imagine the Aegean air and the warmth of the Greek sun; make it happen. Purchase "KOS TRAVEL GUIDE 2024" now and let the journey begin. Your voyage to the picturesque island of Kos awaits, offering a tapestry of experiences that will stay with you long after you've left.

General Information about Kos

Nestled in the lap of the Aegean Sea, Kos appears as a gem in the Dodecanese archipelago, enticing visitors with its timeless appeal and multifaceted attractiveness. As you arrive on this Greek island, let us delve into the basic knowledge that will serve as the basis for your Kos adventure in "KOS TRAVEL GUIDE 2024."

1. Mosaic of History:

1.1 Ancient Legacy:

Explore the island's rich history, filled with stories of past civilizations ranging from the Greeks and Romans to the Byzantines and Ottomans. Kos has an archeological tapestry that includes the renowned

Asklepion, a medicinal refuge built by Hippocrates himself.

1.2 Cultural Collage.

Immerse yourself in the unique cultural tapestry of Kos, where Byzantine, Ottoman and Venetian traditions combine harmoniously with the island's modern vitality. Charming towns, lively marketplaces, and sophisticated resorts present diverse traditions, resulting in a distinct combination of old-world charm and contemporary attraction.

2. Natural Elegance.

2.1 Landscape Symphony:

Kos offers a symphony of scenery, ranging from lush lowlands and olive orchards to steep mountains and gorgeous beaches. Explore lush valleys and learn about the island's biodiversity as nature transforms into an elegant artwork.

2.2 Bathing at Aegean Bliss

Accept the compelling lure of the Aegean Sea. Kos has a variety of beaches, each with its distinct character. Whether you like the colorful energy of teeming beaches or the peaceful calm of secret coves, the island's coastline caters to any beachgoer.

3. Modern Comforts & Island Magic:

3.1 Cosmopolitan Delights.

Experience the ideal combination of contemporary amenities and classic charm. Kos caters to a wide variety of guests, with sophisticated resorts, boutique hotels, and lively markets that reflect the island's modern liveliness.

3.2 Culinary Odyssey:

Take a gourmet trip across Kos' culinary scene. Enjoy authentic Greek cuisine, freshly caught fish, and the island's gastronomic wonders. Every meal, from coastal tavernas to local markets, is a culinary feast.

4. How to Get Here and Around

4.1 Gateway to the Aegean.

"KOS TRAVEL GUIDE 2024" includes crucial information about how to go to Kos, assuring a smooth journey from your starting location to the island's coasts. The book provides information on practical travel alternatives, whether by air or water.

4.2 Island exploration:

Use these practical Kos travel tips to navigate the island easily. From public transit to auto rentals, the book provides the information you need to effectively tour the island, ensuring you don't miss any of its gems.

5. Plan Your Visit:

5.1 Best Time to Unveil Kos:

Discover the best times to visit Kos, each season bringing a unique aspect of the island's appeal. Whether you seek the warmth of summer or the quiet of autumn,

"KOS TRAVEL GUIDE 2024" can help you organize your trip based on your tastes.

5.2 Cultural Etiquettes:

Learn about the local traditions and cultural peculiarities that influence everyday life on the island. Understanding the core of Kos enables you to interact with the community meaningfully, resulting in true bonds throughout your stay.

6. Your Kos Journey Starts Here:

As you read this basic information about Kos, imagine the activities that await you, from ancient ruins to sun-kissed beaches and lively marketplaces to peaceful olive gardens. "KOS TRAVEL GUIDE 2024" sets the setting for an extraordinary voyage, encouraging you to join the island's story. Your Kos adventure starts with each page flip, and the trip is as wonderful as the destination.

Best Time to Visit Kos

Going on an expedition to Kos is about more than simply getting there; it's about creating an experience that connects with the island's specific rhythms, from the subtle rustling of olive fields to the Aegean's relaxing lullaby. In "KOS TRAVEL GUIDE 2024," we weave the fabric of time, directing you to the finest time to visit this wonderful Greek island.

1. Spring Symphony (1.1): Blooms and Beginnings.

Spring marks a vivid rebirth on Kos, with the island bursting into a symphony of color. Olive trees blossom, wildflowers flood the area, and the air starts to warm up gently. Spring is a wonderful season for nature lovers, with lush scenery and pleasant temperatures to explore.

1.2 Cultural Unveiling

Explore the cultural festivals and local celebrations that come to life in spring. Experience Easter customs on the island, which combines religious events, vibrant processions, and a feeling of regeneration in the air.

2. Summer Serenity (2.1 Sun-Drenched Bliss)

Summer on Kos is all about sun-drenched days and pleasant nights. This is the season for beach lovers, as the island's gorgeous beaches welcome you to bask in the Aegean sun. Dive into crystal-clear waters, enjoy water sports, and let the Mediterranean sun create amazing memories.

2.2 Festive vibes:

Enjoy the joyous mood of summer when the island's cities and villages come to life with cultural events, music festivals, and bustling markets. Kos exposes its energetic energy with activities such as visiting ancient sites in the summer heat and eating al fresco by the sea.

3. Autumn tranquility:

3.1 Golden hues and harvest:

As summer ends, fall brings in a season of calm and golden colors. Enjoy pleasant temps, giving it a great time to explore without the intense heat of summer. The island's landscapes take on warm tones, providing a beautiful background for your activities.

3.2 Culinary bounty:

Autumn is a gastronomic joy on Kos, as local markets are brimming with harvest richness. Enjoy the island's culinary delights, from fresh olives and olive oil to seasonal fruits and vegetables. Autumn provides a unique chance to enjoy the tastes of Kos.

4. Winter Retreat:

4.1 Mild winters and seclusion:

Winter on Kos reveals a distinct side of the island: a calm refuge with warm temperatures and fewer tourists, creating an intimate atmosphere. While certain beach activities may be on hold, winter is ideal for individuals seeking isolation and a deeper connection with the island's spirit.

4.2 Cultural Resonance.

Explore historical sights without the summer crowds, immersing yourself in the island's rich history at your speed. Enjoy the quiet mood of winter, with whispering breezes and old ruins providing an exquisite background.

The "KOS TRAVEL GUIDE 2024" lets you pick the period that best suits your trip plans. Whether you desire the vibrant energy of summer, the cultural richness of spring, the calm beauty of autumn, or the hidden refuge of winter, Kos is ready to reveal its riches in any season.

Plan your trip to Kos based on the seasons to create a timeless journey. Purchase "KOS TRAVEL GUIDE 2024" now and flip the pages to discover the finest dates to visit and the moments that will etch themselves into your mind, forging a lasting relationship with this Aegean treasure. Your voyage to Kos awaits, and the island's embrace is ready to unfurl by your preferred schedule.

How to get Around in Kos

In the enchanted embrace of Kos, where ancient history meets sun-kissed beaches, the secret to uncovering the island's richness is how easily you navigate its surroundings. "KOS TRAVEL GUIDE 2024" lends a helping hand to teach you the skill of moving about, ensuring that your trip is more than simply a destination but a smooth exploration of all Kos has to offer.

1. Winged Arrival: 1.1 Kos International Airport.

Your trip begins at Kos International Airport, the island's entryway. The airport, located near the capital, Kos Town, accepts flights from various countries, linking you to the enchantment of the Aegean.

1.2 Airport to Accommodation:

"KOS TRAVEL GUIDE 2024" provides information on hassle-free airport transfers to your hotel. Whether you choose taxis, shuttle services, or auto rentals, our advice will help you begin your Kos adventure with ease and pleasure.

2. Seafarers' Entrances:

2.1 Marine Marvels:

Kos' harbors in Kos Town and Kefalos accept ferries and boats from adjacent islands and the Greek mainland. Arriving by ship provides a stunning start to the island, offering a marine experience even before you foot on land.

2.2 Harbor-to-Hotel:

There are several transportation alternatives available after you arrive at the pier. Discover the finest routes from the port to your preferred destination, whether it's a popular resort or a hidden treasure on the island.

3. Island on Wheels: 3.1 Rental Cars:

Car rentals serve as a passport to new territory for free spirits keen to explore every nook of Kos at their speed. "KOS TRAVEL GUIDE 2024" offers advice on hiring a vehicle, allowing you to explore and discover the island's hidden beauties.

3.2 Public Transit:

Using public transit allows you to get immersed in the local rhythm. Buses and taxis run across the island, providing a simple and affordable means to get between towns, beaches, and historical sites.

4. Two-Wheel Adventure:

4.1 Biking Bliss:

Enjoy the beauty of Kos on two wheels. Discover lovely bike lanes, whether along the coast or through little towns. The book highlights bike rental alternatives, laying the groundwork for an environmentally responsible and unhurried journey.

4.2 Moped and Scooter:

Discover the excitement of riding around the island on a moped or scooter. These agile choices, ideal for short distances and beach hopping, provide an exciting element to your Kos vacation.

5. Walking Through History: 5.1 Exploration on Foot:

Many of Kos' historical and cultural treasures are located nearby. "KOS TRAVEL GUIDE 2024" promotes unhurried exploration on foot by suggesting walking tours that enable you to absorb the island's rich tapestry at your speed.

5.2 Guided tours:

For those looking for customized experiences, guided tours provide a detailed overview of Kos' attractions. The book recommends reliable tour providers, ensuring your trip is enriched with insights from informed local guides.

Your Kos journey awaits.

In "KOS TRAVEL GUIDE 2024," traveling about Kos is more than simply a mode of transportation; it's an essential aspect of your journey. Purchase the book now and let the pages unfurl into a seamless trip in which every method of transportation serves as a vessel for fresh discoveries. Your Kos journey is waiting for you: it's easy, bright, and eager to be explored!

Top Things To Do in Kos

Kos, located in the center of the Aegean Sea, beckons with a mix of experiences beyond the ordinary. "KOS TRAVEL GUIDE 2024" encourages you to immerse yourself in the island's charm by discovering the best things to do - a carefully picked symphony of activities that guarantee to make your Kos trip a memorable song.

1. Journey across time:

1.1 Asklepion Exploration.

Follow in Hippocrates' footsteps and visit Asklepion, a historic healing sanctuary. "KOS TRAVEL GUIDE 2024" reveals the mysteries of this historical monument, leading you through its columns, temples, and old halls reverberating with the sounds of ancient healing.

1.2 Castle of Knights:

Ascend to the Castle of the Knights in Kos Town, where ancient walls meet panoramic vistas. Dive into the island's history as your guide leads you inside this renowned stronghold, which testifies to Kos's existence as a crossroads of civilizations.

2. Beach Bliss and Watersports: 2.1 Therma Beach Retreat.

Relax in the therapeutic embrace of Therma Beach, where natural hot springs meet the Aegean Sea. "KOS TRAVEL GUIDE 2024" describes the revitalizing pleasure of bathing in warm waters while waves wash against the coast.

2.2 Kardamena's Sand Playground:

Kardamena is a beach lover's paradise. Discover the bright spirit of this resort town, which has golden beaches, water sports, and a bustling waterfront. The book directs you to the greatest areas for sunbathing, swimming, and beachfront activities.

3. Culinary Odyssey: 3.1 Adventures at Local Markets

Exploring local markets allows you to get immersed in Kos' gastronomic tapestry. "KOS TRAVEL GUIDE 2024" takes you to crowded marketplaces where the scent of fresh vegetables, spices, and local delicacies entices the senses.

3.2 Taverna Delights:

Enjoy the island's culinary delights in traditional tavernas. From grilled octopus to moussaka, the book explains where to get traditional Greek tastes, ensuring that each meal celebrates Kos' culinary history.

4. Island Cycling Exploration:

4.1 Bike Adventures:

Feel the breeze in your hair as you explore Kos on two wheels. "KOS TRAVEL GUIDE 2024" reveals gorgeous cycling lanes that take you past olive trees, seaside footpaths, and picturesque towns. Discover the delight of eco-friendly discovery with carefully planned bike routes.

4.2 Magnificent Asclepiades Forest:

Take a nature-filled cycling adventure in the Asclepiades Forest. Allow the guide to walk you to the center of this beautiful oasis, where shaded pathways and the symphony of bird music provide a peaceful respite.

5. Sunset Strolls and Nightlife: 5.1 Zia's Magical Sunsets

Experience the grandeur of a Kos sunset at Zia, a town on Dikaios Mountain. "KOS TRAVEL GUIDE 2024" directs you to the ideal viewing spots where the sun colors the sky orange and pink, creating a heavenly sight.

5.2 Kos Town Nightlife:

When the sun goes down, Kos Town comes alive with exciting nightlife. Discover the island's modern energy as the tour takes you to bustling taverns, seaside tavernas, and colorful squares where the night is filled with music and laughter.

6. Windsurfing Adventure:

6.1 Mastichari's Windy Playground:

Windsurfing is a popular activity in Mastichari. The tour leads you around this windswept paradise, offering information on rentals, instruction, and the greatest sites for windsurfing thrills.

6.2 Kite Surfing in Psalidi:

Psalidi develops as a kite surfing hotspot. "KOS TRAVEL GUIDE 2024" delves into the thrilling world of kite surfing, leading you through the fundamentals, best sites, and where to find the ideal combination of wind and waves.

7. Cultural Connections:

7.1 Hippocrates Museum:

Explore the life of Hippocrates at the Hippocratic Museum in Kos Town. "KOS TRAVEL GUIDE 2024" delves into the history of medicine, including relics and displays honoring the island's famous character.

7.2 Casa Romana.

Discover the splendor of Casa Romana, a Roman house with beautiful mosaics and paintings. The guide will accompany you around this archeological marvel, revealing insights into ancient Kos' everyday life.

8. Hidden Gems and Local Secrets:

8.1 Agios Stefanos Beach Caves:

Go off the main road to Agios Stefanos Beach, where secret caverns await exploration. "KOS TRAVEL GUIDE 2024" will take you to this remote refuge, where turquoise seas and natural caverns form a peaceful respite.

8.2 Kefalos Cliff Views:

Seek panoramic views in Kefalos, where the cliffs provide a spectacular perspective of the Aegean Sea. The guide directs you to the greatest vistas, allowing you to capture the spirit of Kos' natural beauty.

Your Symphony and Your Kos Experience:

In "KOS TRAVEL GUIDE 2024," these best things to do are more than simply activities; they are notes in a symphony, ready to be played as you create your song on the island. Purchase the book today and let the magical sensations of Kos speak to your spirit. Your Kos symphony is waiting for you, bright and harmonic, ready to be arranged!

Best Beaches On Kos

The beaches of Kos, Greece, are among the most gorgeous in the Dodecanese islands. The majority of Kos beaches are sandy, with clear blue seas. Many Kos beaches, such as Kardamena, Agios Stefanos, Kefalos, and Lambi, are organized and well-equipped for tourists, while others are remote and popular with naturists. Below is a list of the top beaches on Kos Island.

Aside from the beaches, there are other destinations for sightseeing.

Kos Mastichari Beach

Mastichari Beach Kos is 27 kilometers south of Kos town and 3 kilometers northwest of Antimachia. The pristine beach and green seas provide the ideal exotic scene.

There are many colorful loungers and umbrellas in the center of the beach and various water sports amenities. A lengthy tuft of trees adorns the surrounding region, providing an ideal site for pleasant shade.

The village is built around the natural harbor and provides various tourist services such as lodging, restaurants, cafés, and shopping. It is generally busy throughout the day. The village's tiny port provides regular connections to the island of Kalymnos.

Kos Thermes Beach

Thermes Beach on Kos is one of the most gorgeous spots to visit. It is approximately 12 kilometers from Kos town. When you arrive, several spots to relax and drink are near the parking lot.

Kos Agios Stefanos Beach

Agios Stefanos Beach Kos is 40 kilometers southwest of Kos town and 3 kilometers northeast of Kefalos. The rocky landscape around Agios Stefanos is covered with lovely flowers and luxuriant flora. The beach is composed of sand and stones.

The remnants of historic Christian temples may be located nearby, providing a magnificent backdrop for your photography. However, the most remarkable element of the region is Kastri, a little islet that serves as a barren fortress amid the sea.

All of these aspects are ingeniously blended to provide a pleasant experience for guests. The seas are shallow, and numerous umbrellas line the beachfront, offering enough shade.

Kos Kardamena Beach

Kardamena Beach Kos: Kardamena Beach is one of the greatest places to swim and sunbathe. It is situated 30 kilometers southwest of Kos town, in front of the tourist resort. The beach is coated with smooth sand and extends more than three kilometers to the port. Its magnificent clear seas draw many people, and loungers and umbrellas are provided along the shore. Kardamena is a popular destination for visitors and Greek travelers due to its improved infrastructure. The community provides a variety of rooms and contemporary conveniences to ensure a comfortable holiday.

Where to Stay in Kos
OKU Kos.

The adults-only OKU Kos, located on the sandy beach 4 kilometers from Marmari Village in Kos, is a village-style hotel with an outdoor pool and a contemporary restaurant set in well-kept grounds. Guests may relax in the on-site spa, which includes an indoor pool and a hammam, or work out at the fitness center.

A flat-screen TV with satellite channels, a DVD player, and a CD player are included. Some rooms have a sitting space for your convenience. The room has a coffee machine. Every room comes with a private bathroom. Extras include bathrobes, slippers and complimentary toiletries.

Guests may begin their day with a buffet breakfast offered daily in the on-site restaurant, which also serves nutritious, regionally inspired meals for lunch and supper.

Yoga classes may be scheduled on the outdoor yoga terrace, and other outdoor activities such as stand-up paddling, horseback riding, and trips can be planned. There is a 24-hour front desk and a gift store on the site.

Kos Town is 13 kilometers from OKU Kos, while Kos International "Hippocrates" Airport is 10 kilometers distant. On-site amenities include free WiFi and private parking.

Most popular amenities.

Outdoor swimming pool. Beachfront, Free WiFi

Airport Shuttle, Spa & Wellness Centre, Nonsmoking rooms. Fitness center, Bar Private beach area. Fabulous breakfast.

Address

SIKAMINI STR, Marmari, 85300, Greece.

Blue Lagoon City Hotel

You are qualified for the Genius discount at Blue Lagoon City Hotel! To save money at this resort, just sign in.

Blue Lagoon City Hotel is centrally situated in Kos Town, barely 200 meters from the harbor. It has a swimming pool, a poolside bar-restaurant, and a spa section with a gym and an indoor pool. It also has a lobby bar and a large restaurant that serves buffet breakfast.

Blue Lagoon's rooms and suites are air-conditioned and have a fridge, electric kettle, and television. The private bathroom has a shower and a hairdryer.

Guests may rest on the sun loungers near the pool, while children can swim securely in their own pool. The comfortable lounge space has two TV areas.

Snacks are available for lunch in the pool bar-restaurant, and supper is provided à la carte in the main restaurant. Drinks, drinks, and coffee are offered at the pool and the lobby bar.

Blue Lagoon City Hotel offers bicycle and automobile rental services.

Address

 El. Venizelou 73, Kos Town, 85300, Greece.

Nicolas Grand Suites

Nicolas Grand Suites, Adults Only is located in Kardamaina and has a seasonal outdoor swimming pool, exercise center, shared lounge, and restaurant. This four-star hotel has a business center and a concierge service. The motel has a 24-hour front desk, airport shuttles, room service, and free WiFi throughout.

The hotel's rooms have air conditioning, a desk, a balcony with a mountain view, a private bathroom, a flat-screen TV, bed linen, and towels. Nicolas Grand Suites, Adults Only has several apartments with sea views, and all suites have balconies. All rooms will have a closet and a kettle.

The hotel provides a buffet or continental breakfast.

Nicolas Grand Suites, Adults Only is located 1.3 kilometers from Kardamena Beach and 3.7 kilometers from Antimachia Castle. Kos International Airport is 9 kilometers from the hotel.

Most popular amenities.

Outdoor swimming pool. Free WiFi, Free parking

Nonsmoking rooms. Airport shuttle Fitness center

Room service, Tea/coffee maker in every room.

Bar and breakfast options.

Address

Kardamena 853 02, Kardamaina, 85302, Greece.

Printed in Great Britain
by Amazon

42482817R00030